Collins
New
Primary
Maths

Assisting
Maths
Discussion Book 2

Peter Clarke

William Collins' dream of knowledge for all began with the publication of his first book in 1819.
A self-educated mill worker, he not only enriched millions of lives, but also founded a
flourishing publishing house. Today, staying true to this spirit, Collins books are packed with
inspiration, innovation and practical expertise. They place you at the centre of a world of
possibility and give you exactly what you need to explore it.

Collins. Freedom to teach.

Published by Collins
An imprint of HarperCollinsPublishers
77-85 Fulham Palace Road
Hammersmith
London
W6 8JB

Browse the complete Collins Education catalogue at
www.collinseducation.com

10 9 8 7 6 5 4 3 2 1

ISBN 978-0-00-722119-6

British Library Cataloguing in Publication Data

A Catalogue record for this publication is available from the British Library

Cover design by Laing and Carroll
Series design by Neil Adams
Cover artwork by Jon Stuart
Internal design by Steve Evans and Mark Walker Design
Illustrations by Steve Evans
Edited by Fiona Lazenby
Proofread by Jan Fisher
Picture researcher: Fran Vargo

Acknowledgements
The author wishes to thank Brian Molyneaux for his valuable contribution to this publication.

Photos
Page 4: David Towersey. Page 5: David Towersey. Page 11: Dreamstime.com: top left, Peter Guess; centre right above, Chrswbrwn; centre right below, Marcel
Krol; bottom left, Paul Fleet; Fotolia.com: centre left below, Patricia Hofmeester; bottom centre, Sharpshot; iStockphoto: centre, Andrew Rich; Leo Reynolds
www.flickr.com/lwr: top right, centre left above. Page 12: Dreamstime.com: centre above, Sergey Kubyshin; centre left below, Hunter Wagstaff; Leo
Reynolds www.flickr.com/lwr: top left, top centre, centre right below; David Towersey: top right. Page 13: Dreamstime.com: centre left above, Dave Cordina;
top right, Hunk; Fotolia.com: bottom left, jon11; iStockphoto: centre right above, Angelika Stern; Leo Reynolds www.flickr.com/lwr: top left, top centre.
Page 26: David Towersey. Page 27: David Towersey. Page 30: David Towersey. Page 31: David Towersey. Page 70: Dreamstime.com: top left, Branislav Ostojic;
top centre, Sharpshot; top right, Irochka; centre left above, Marcus Miranda; centre, Spe; centre right above, Fatih Kocyildir; centre right, Sergey Peterman;
centre left below, Piotr Adamski; centre right below, Christophe Testi; bottom centre, Tombaky; bottom right, Paulpaladin; Leo Reynolds
www.flickr.com/lwr: bottom left. Page 71: Department of Defense: centre right above; Dreamstime.com:top centre, Jamalludin Bin Abu Seman Din; top
right, Stepan Popov; centre left, Icefields; centre, Noam Armonn; bottom centre, Kitsen; bottom right, Design56; Leo Reynolds www.flickr.com/lwr: top left,
centre right below, bottom left.

Printed and bound by Printing Express, Hong Kong

Contents

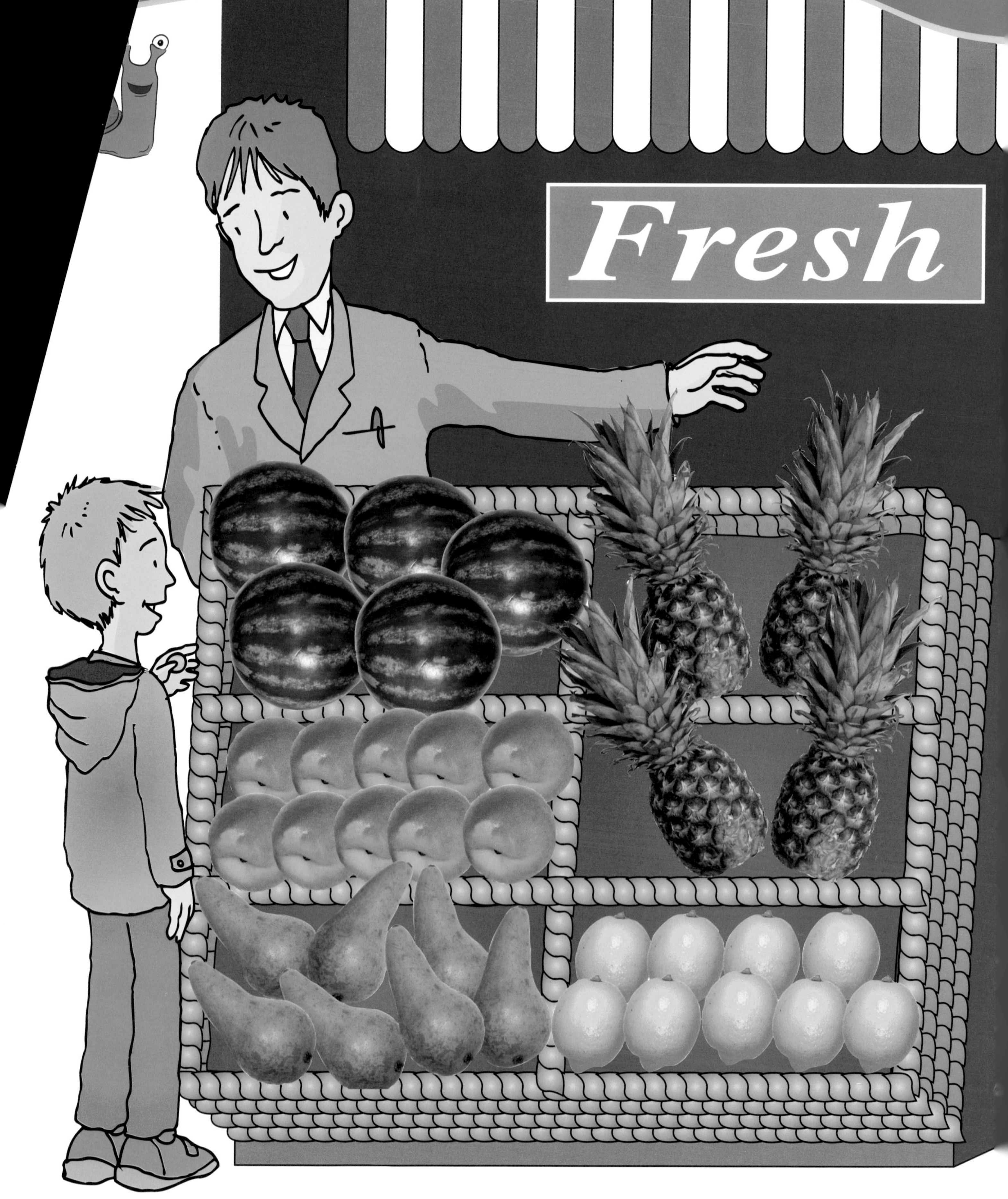
Fresh

Fruit

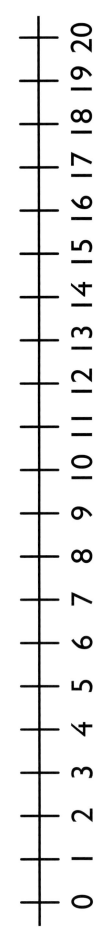

0 1 2 3 4 5 6 7 8 9 10 11 12 13 14 15 16 17 18 19 20

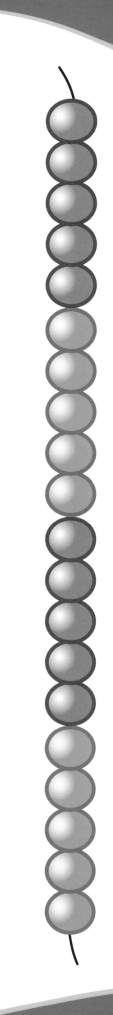

10   20   30   40   50   60   70   80   90   100

1	2	3	4	5	6	7	8	9	10
11	12	13	14	15	16	17	18	19	20
21	22	23	24	25	26	27	28	29	30
31	32	33	34	35	36	37	38	39	40
41	42	43	44	45	46	47	48	49	50
51	52	53	54	55	56	57	58	59	60
61	62	63	64	65	66	67	68	69	70
71	72	73	74	75	76	77	78	79	80
81	82	83	84	85	86	87	88	89	90
91	92	93	94	95	96	97	98	99	100

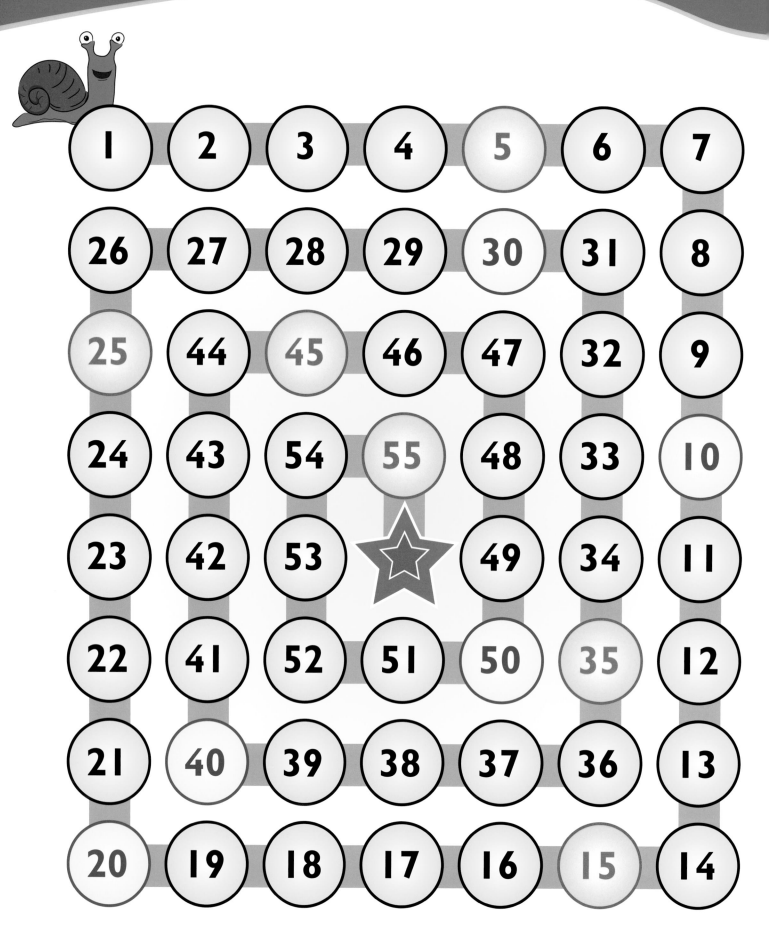

three 7

16

Level 7

ONE WAY

9

14

5
Check-in

six

4

10

 £1.00

 20ᵖ

 10ᵖ

38

fifty-nine

30

eighty-two

forty-seven

069244

41.6 4

km/h
MPH

60 80 100

40 100

20 120

135

ONE HUNDRED
POTTERGATE

thirty

Fun Size Apples
7 Pack
WAS 79p
59p

Parsnips 500g
39p

Mango Each
39p

Onions 1kg
WAS 49p
29p

137

13 days
£**949**
from
per person

263

7 1 2

two hundred and thirty-eight

five hundred

1000 PUZZLE

BUS STOP

Lordship Park

towards
Newington Green

141 341

was £945
Now only
£699*

nine hundred
and forty six

Two-digit numbers

A game for 2 players

You need:
- pencil and paper clip, for the spinners
- counters in two different colours

Before you start:
- Each player choose a set of coloured counters.

Take turns to:
- spin both spinners
- put the two numbers together to make a two-digit number
- say the number you have made
- place one of your counters on that number on the grid.

Rule:
- If a number has already got a counter on it, have another go.

- The winner is the first player to get 3 of their counters in a line. A line can go sideways, up or down, or diagonally.

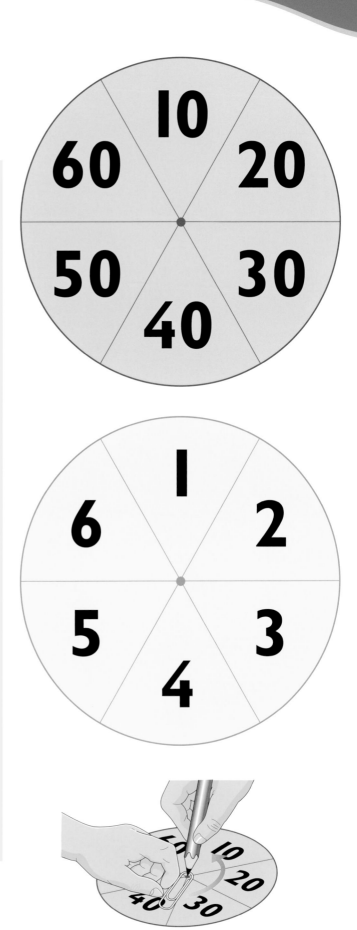

35	14	45	23	54	15
25	62	53	12	31	46
13	61	44	52	63	26
34	51	24	32	16	43
22	41	36	66	55	64
56	11	65	21	33	42

38

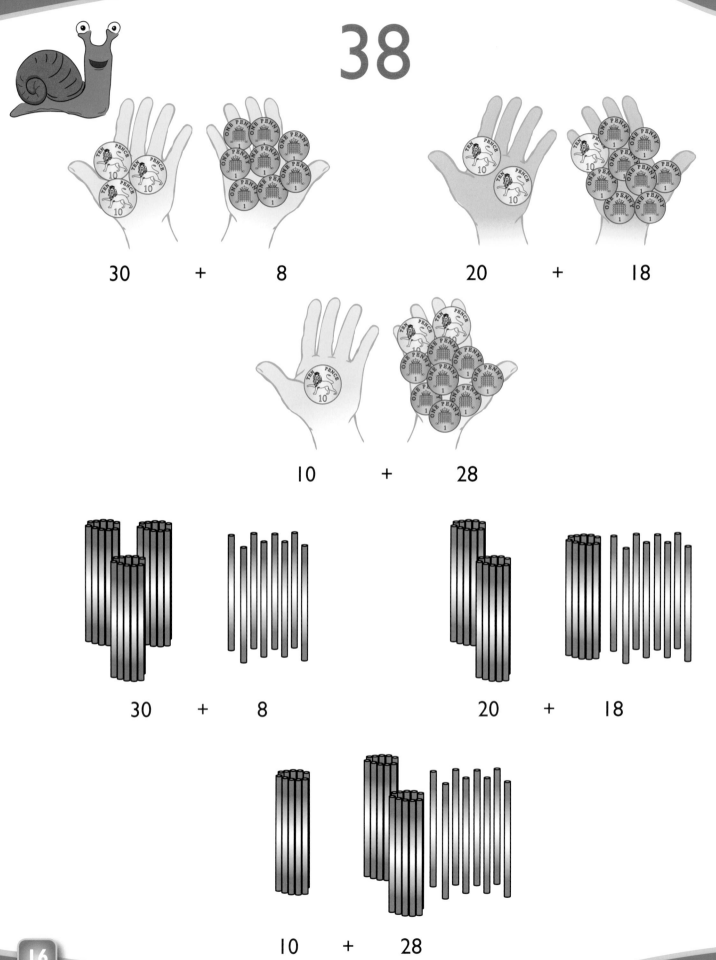

30   +   8   20   +   18

10   +   28

30   +   8   20   +   18

10   +   28

38

30 + 8

20 + 18

10 + 28

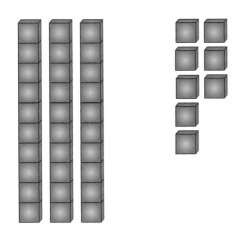

30 + 8

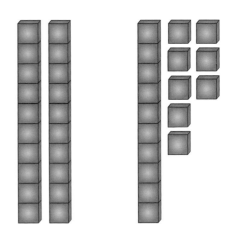

20 + 18

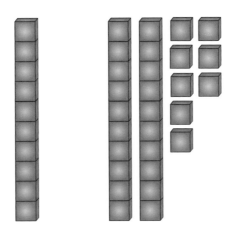

10 + 28

63

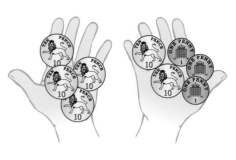

60 + 3   50 + 13   40 + 23

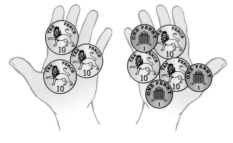

30 + 33   20 + 43   10 + 53

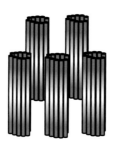
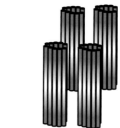

60 + 3   50 + 13   40 + 23

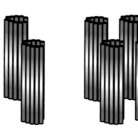

30 + 33   20 + 43   10 + 53

63

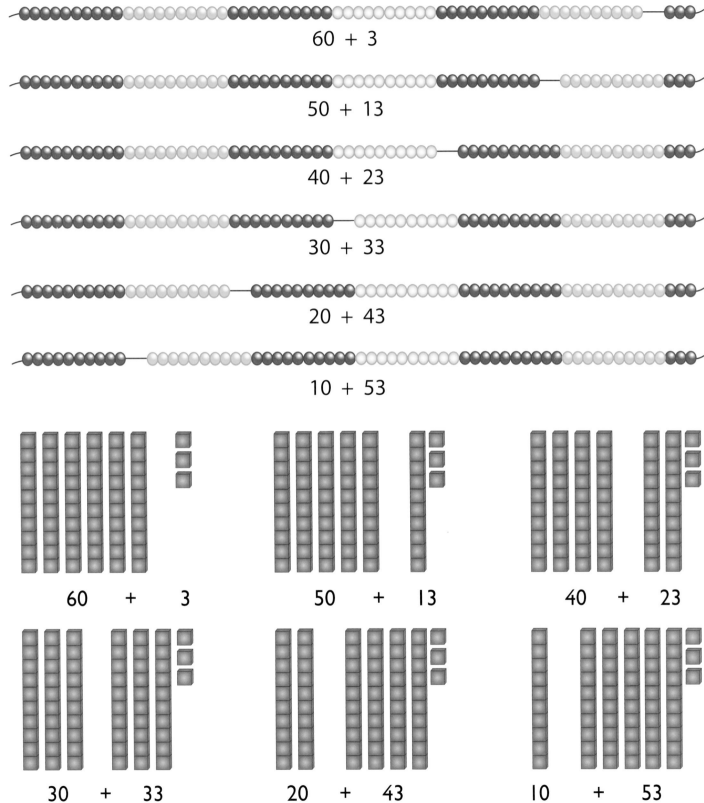

60 + 3

50 + 13

40 + 23

30 + 33

20 + 43

10 + 53

60 + 3

50 + 13

40 + 23

30 + 33

20 + 43

10 + 53

90	80	70	60	50	40	30	20	10
9	8	7	6	5	4	3	2	1

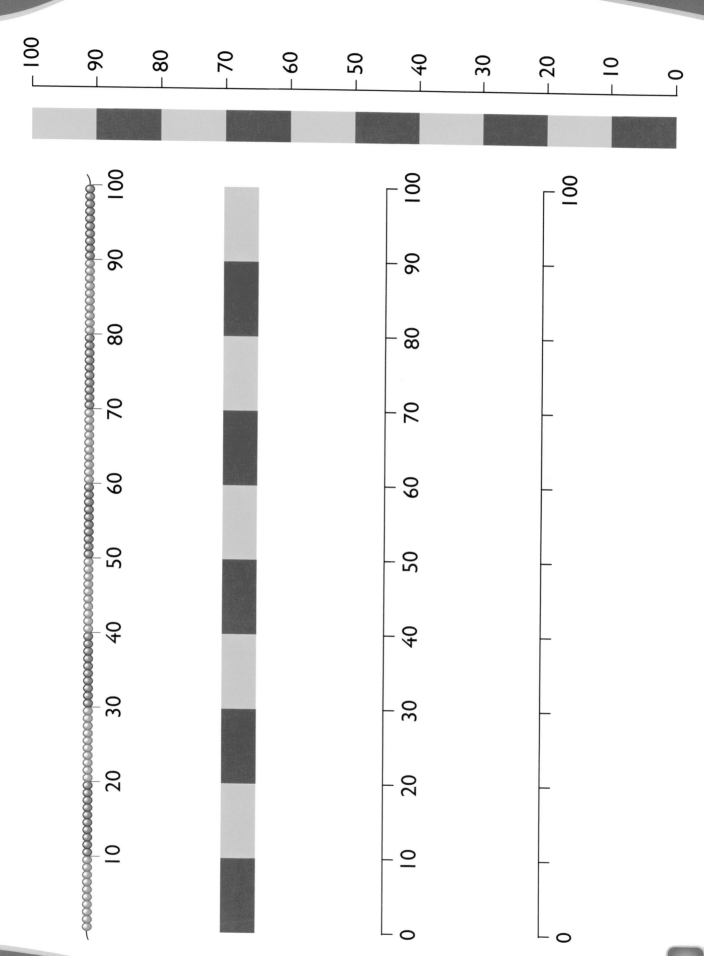

More or less

A game for 2 players

You need:
- pencil and paper clip, for the spinner
- 2 counters, each a different colour

Before you start:
- Each player choose a counter.
- Put your counter on

Take turns to:
- spin the spinner and say the word.

Rules:
- If you spin 'more', 'bigger', 'larger' or 'greater', move one plank in any direction to a number that is larger than the number you are on.
- If you spin 'less', 'smaller' or 'lower', move one plank in any direction to a number that is smaller than the number you are on.
- If you can't move, miss a go.

- The winner is the first player to reach

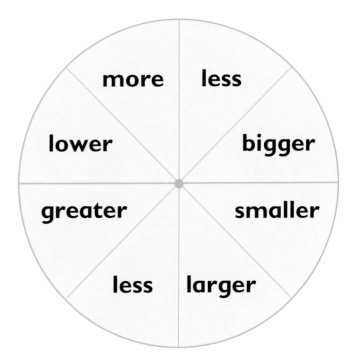

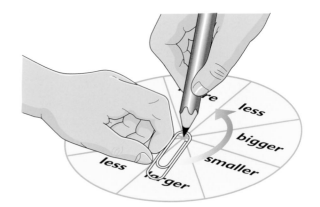

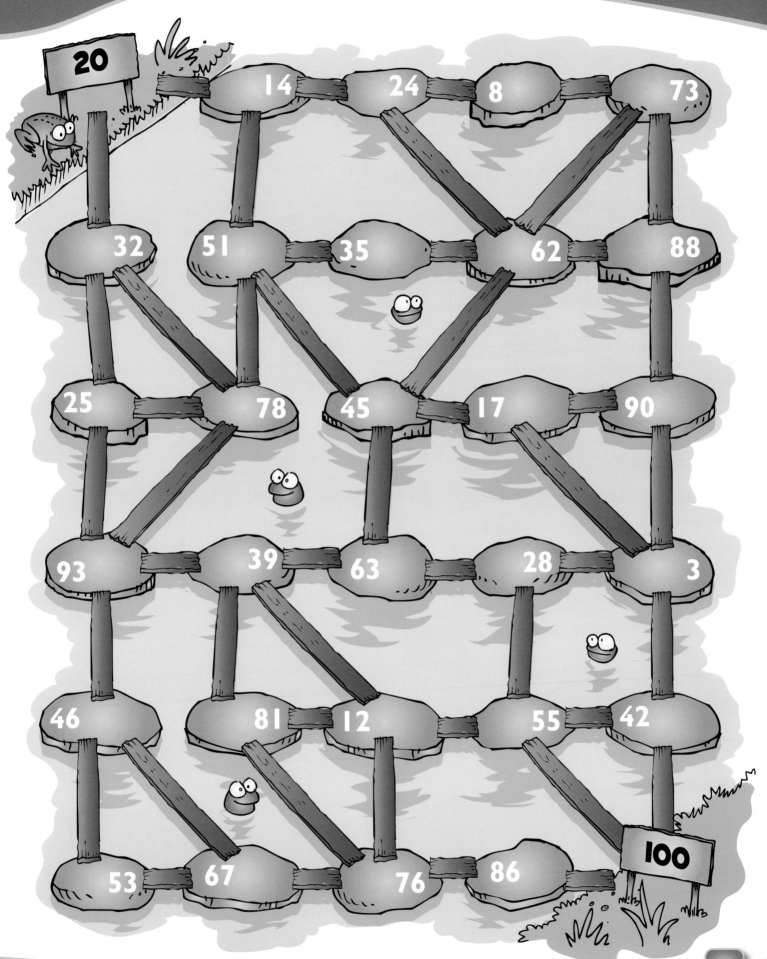

More than or less than

A game for 2 players

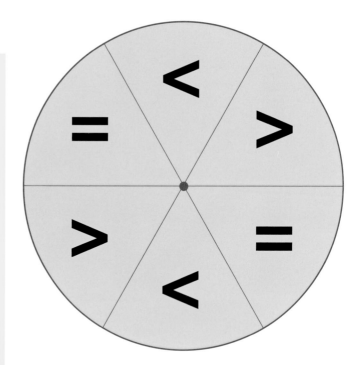

You need:
- 1–20 dice
- pencil and paper clip, for the spinner
- counters in two different colours

Before you start:
- Each player choose a set of coloured counters.

Take turns to:
- roll the dice

- spin the spinner

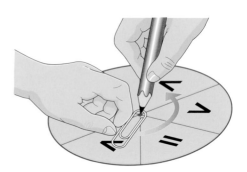

- choose a number on the grid to end the statement

- cover that number with a counter and say the statement.

16 is less than 33

Rules:
- You can only cover one number each go.
- If you can't go, miss that turn.

- The winner is the first player to get 4 of their counters in a line. A line can go sideways, up or down, or diagonally.

11	42	19	4	35	24	13
23	2	15	29	43	1	45
9	31	25	6	21	32	28
27	38	36	30	18	47	8
14	33	12	40	3	16	22
5	48	26	17	44	46	37
39	20	7	34	41	10	49

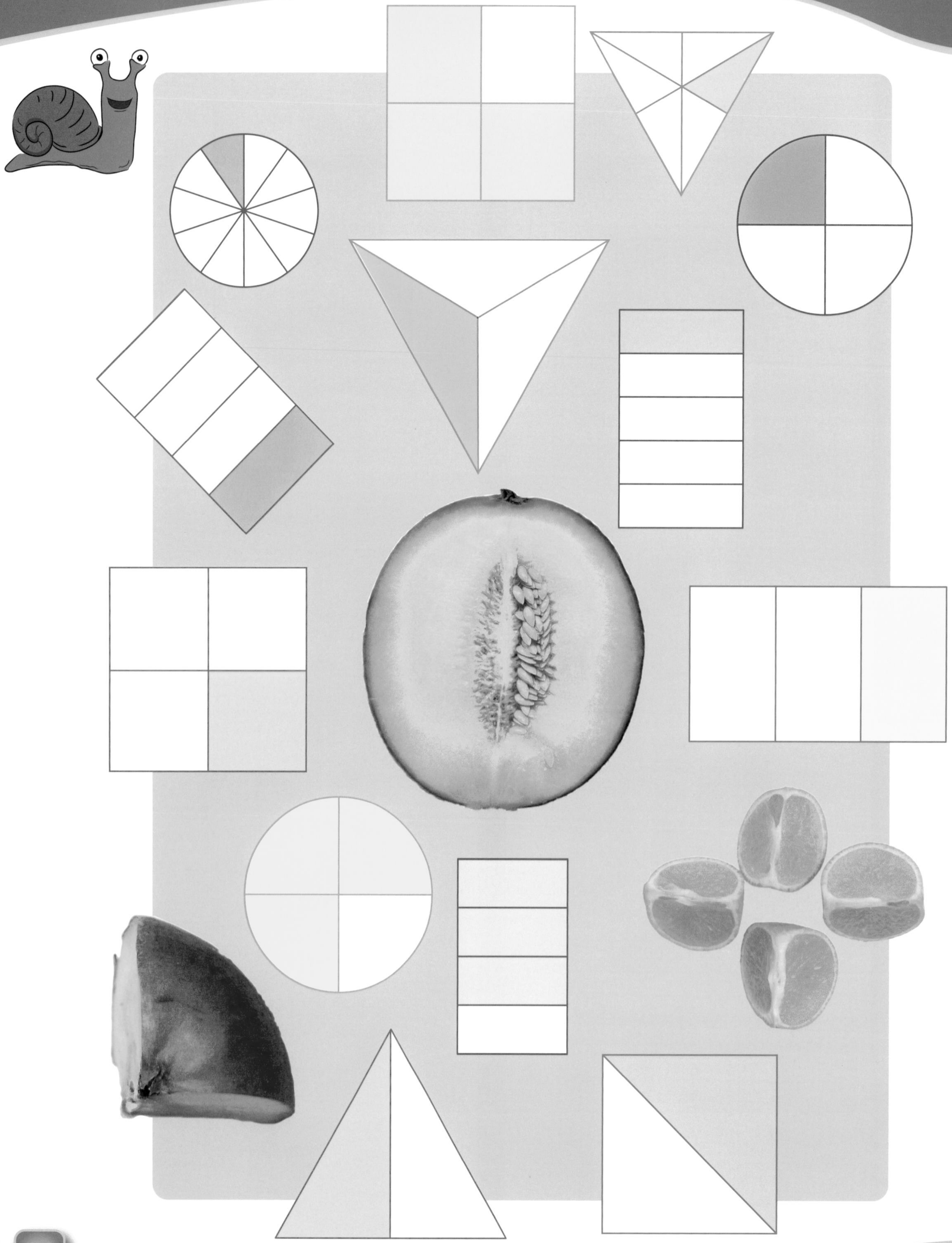

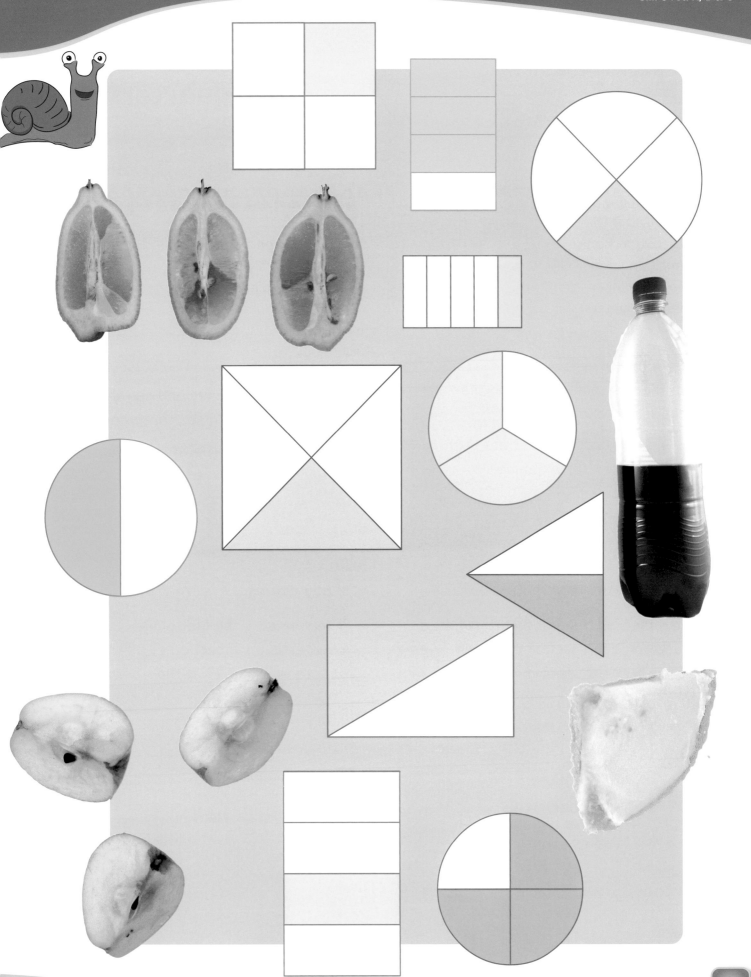

Half and one-quarter game

A game for 2 players

You need:
- Discussion Book
- pencil and paper clip, for the spinner
- pile of counters

Take turns to:
- spin the red spinner and say the fraction, for example, 'half'
- cover this fraction of a shape with your counters, for example

Rule:
- If you can't go, miss that turn.
- The winner is the first player to put a counter in each section of all the shapes on page 29 of their book.

Half and quarters game

A game for 2 players

You need:
- Discussion Book
- pencil and paper clip, for the spinner
- pile of counters

Take turns to:
- spin the blue spinner and say the fraction, for example, 'three-quarters'
- cover this fraction of a shape with your counters, for example

Rule:
- If you can't go, miss that turn.
- The winner is the first player to put a counter in each section of all the shapes on page 29 of their book.

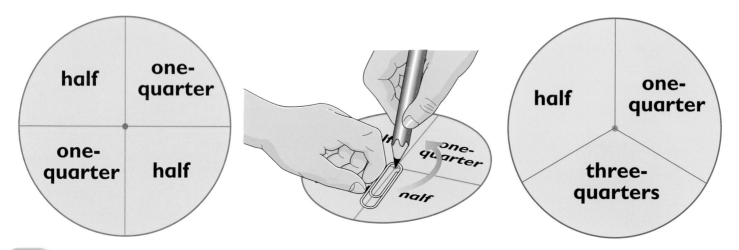

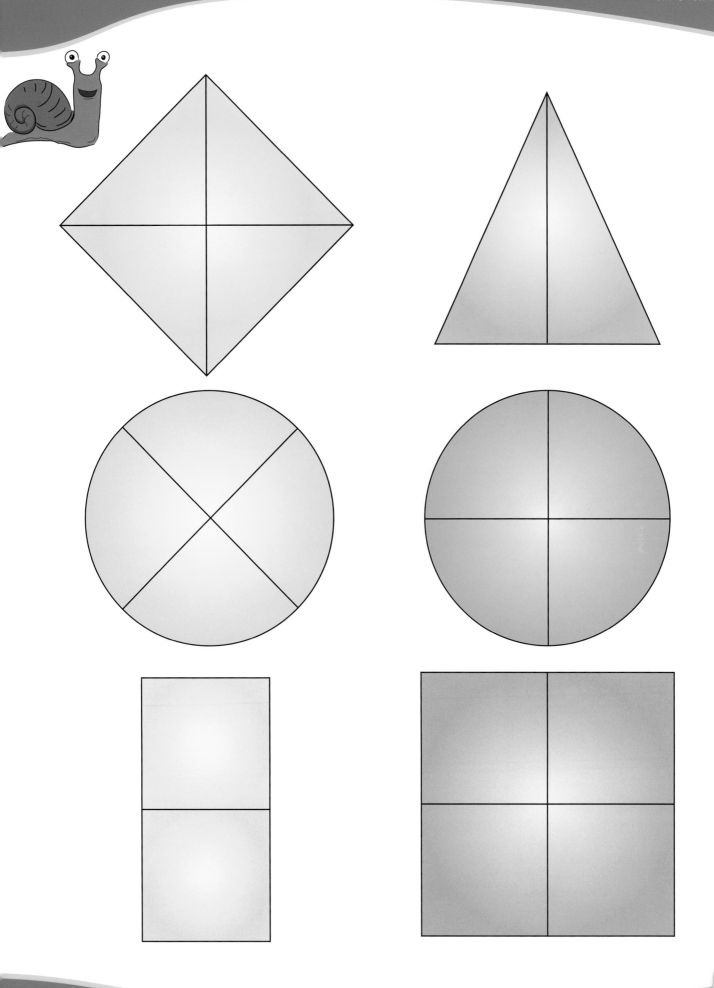

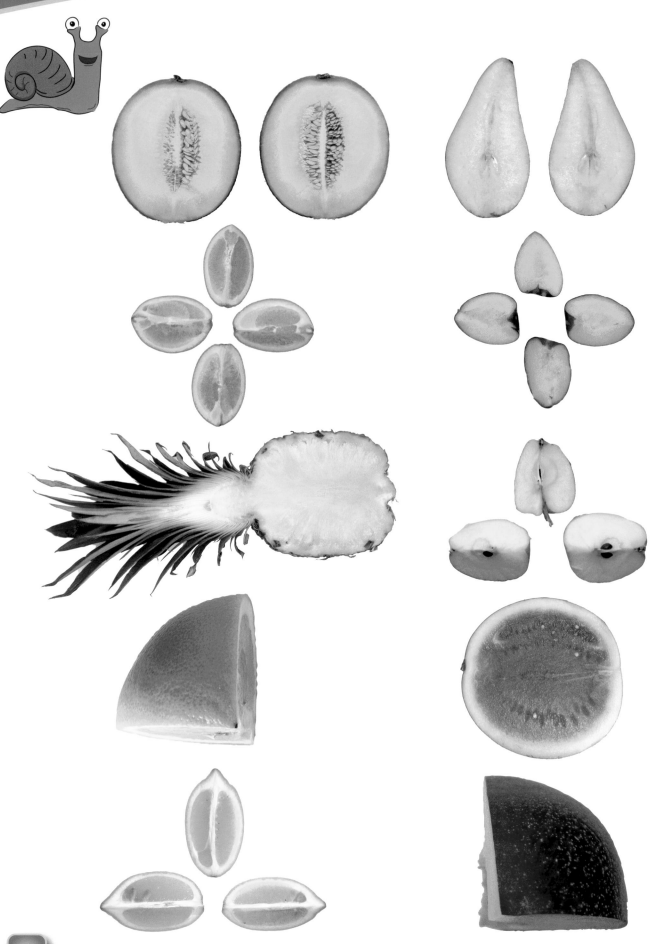

Addition and subtraction number facts for 2

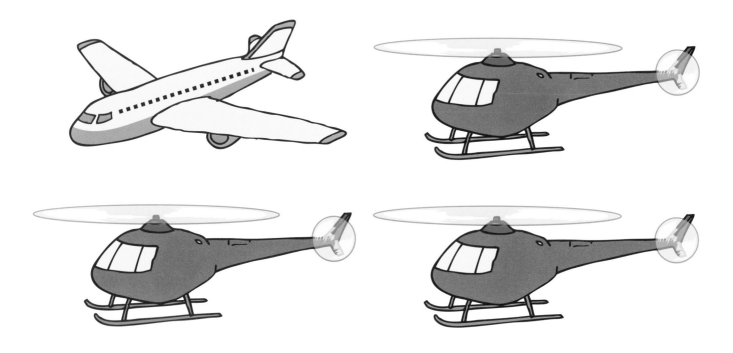

Addition and subtraction number facts for 3

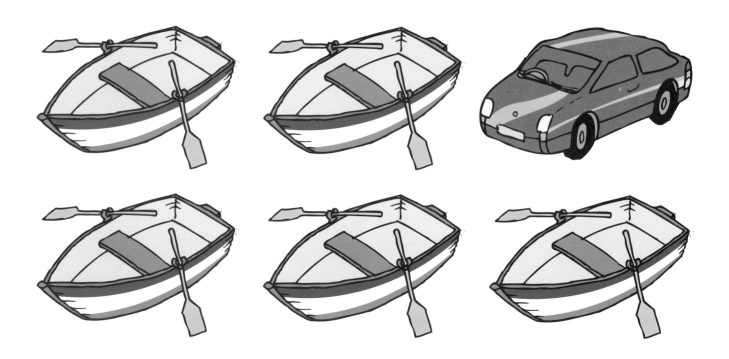

Addition and subtraction number facts for 4

Addition and subtraction number facts for 5

Addition and subtraction number facts for 6

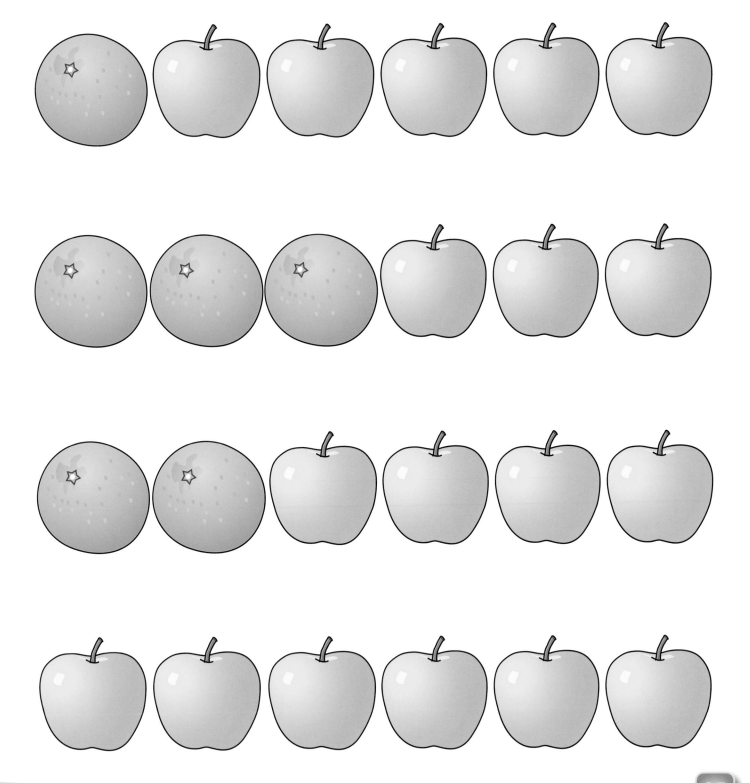

Addition and subtraction number facts for 7

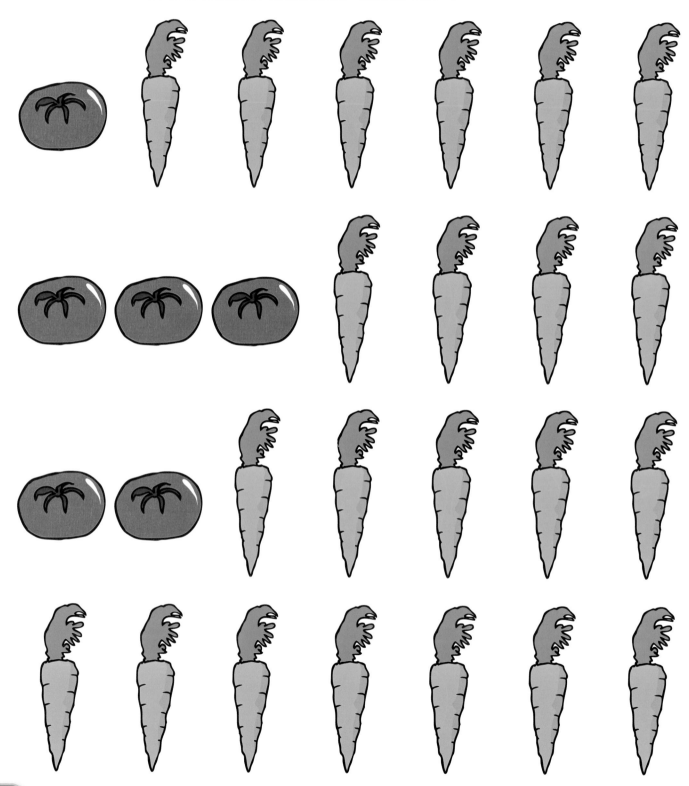

Addition and subtraction number facts for 8

Addition and subtraction number facts for 9

Addition and subtraction number facts for 10

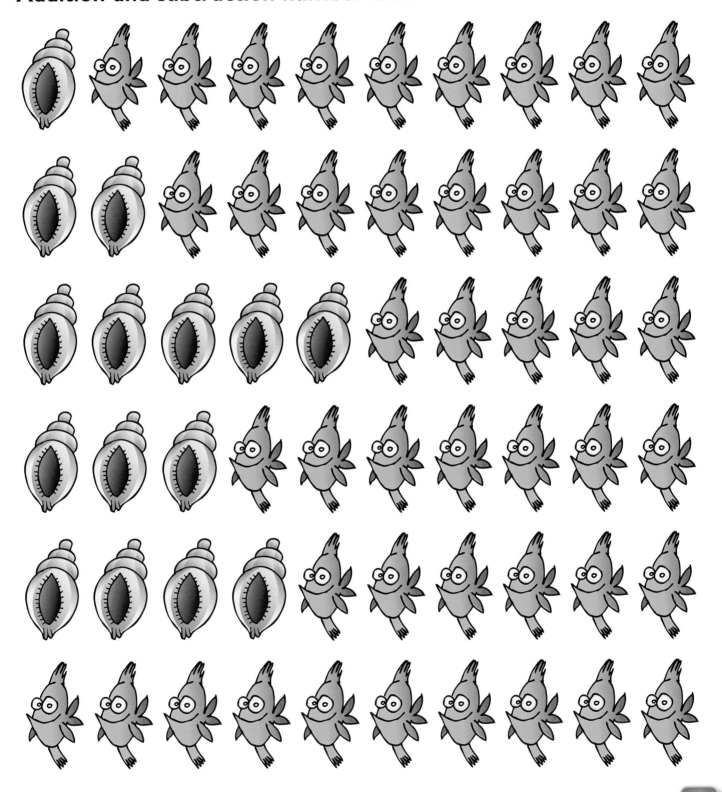

Addition and subtraction number facts to 10

Number facts for 0

0 + 0 = 0	0 − 0 = 0

Number facts for 1

1 + 0 = 1	1 − 0 = 1
0 + 1 = 1	1 − 1 = 0

Number facts for 2

2 + 0 = 2	2 − 0 = 2
1 + 1 = 2	2 − 1 = 1
0 + 2 = 2	2 − 2 = 0

Number facts for 3

3 + 0 = 3	3 − 0 = 3
2 + 1 = 3	3 − 1 = 2
1 + 2 = 3	3 − 2 = 1
0 + 3 = 3	3 − 3 = 0

Number facts for 4

4 + 0 = 4	4 − 0 = 4
3 + 1 = 4	4 − 1 = 3
2 + 2 = 4	4 − 2 = 2
1 + 3 = 4	4 − 3 = 1
0 + 4 = 4	4 − 4 = 0

Number facts for 5

5 + 0 = 5	5 − 0 = 5
4 + 1 = 5	5 − 1 = 4
3 + 2 = 5	5 − 2 = 3
2 + 3 = 5	5 − 3 = 2
1 + 4 = 5	5 − 4 = 1
0 + 5 = 5	5 − 5 = 0

Number facts for 6

6 + 0 = 6	6 − 0 = 6
5 + 1 = 6	6 − 1 = 5
4 + 2 = 6	6 − 2 = 4
3 + 3 = 6	6 − 3 = 3
2 + 4 = 6	6 − 4 = 2
1 + 5 = 6	6 − 5 = 1
0 + 6 = 6	6 − 6 = 0

Number facts for 7

7 + 0 = 7	7 − 0 = 7
6 + 1 = 7	7 − 1 = 6
5 + 2 = 7	7 − 2 = 5
4 + 3 = 7	7 − 3 = 4
3 + 4 = 7	7 − 4 = 3
2 + 5 = 7	7 − 5 = 2
1 + 6 = 7	7 − 6 = 1
0 + 7 = 7	7 − 7 = 0

Number facts for 8

8 + 0 = 8	8 − 0 = 8
7 + 1 = 8	8 − 1 = 7
6 + 2 = 8	8 − 2 = 6
5 + 3 = 8	8 − 3 = 5
4 + 4 = 8	8 − 4 = 4
3 + 5 = 8	8 − 5 = 3
2 + 6 = 8	8 − 6 = 2
1 + 7 = 8	8 − 7 = 1
0 + 8 = 8	8 − 8 = 0

Number facts for 9

9 + 0 = 9	9 − 0 = 9
8 + 1 = 9	9 − 1 = 8
7 + 2 = 9	9 − 2 = 7
6 + 3 = 9	9 − 3 = 6
5 + 4 = 9	9 − 4 = 5
4 + 5 = 9	9 − 5 = 4
3 + 6 = 9	9 − 6 = 3
2 + 7 = 9	9 − 7 = 2
1 + 8 = 9	9 − 8 = 1
0 + 9 = 9	9 − 9 = 0

Number facts for 10

10 + 0 = 10	10 − 0 = 10
9 + 1 = 10	10 − 1 = 9
8 + 2 = 10	10 − 2 = 8
7 + 3 = 10	10 − 3 = 7
6 + 4 = 10	10 − 4 = 6
5 + 5 = 10	10 − 5 = 5
4 + 6 = 10	10 − 6 = 4
3 + 7 = 10	10 − 7 = 3
2 + 8 = 10	10 − 8 = 2
1 + 9 = 10	10 − 9 = 1
0 + 10 = 10	10 − 10 = 0

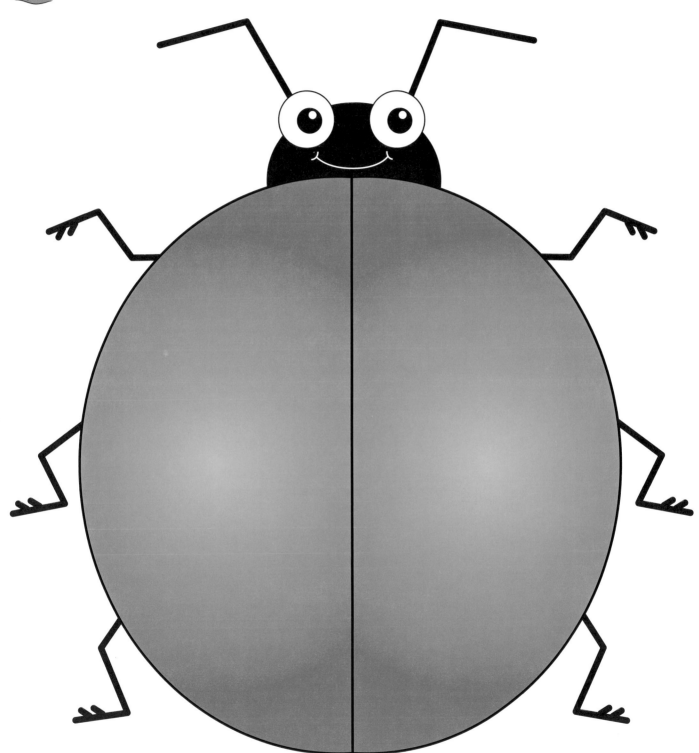

Add the dice

A game for 2 players

You need:
- two 1–6 dice
- counters in two different colours

Before you start:
- Each player choose a set of coloured counters.

Take turns to:
- roll the dice
- add the two numbers and say the answer

> 5 add 2 equals 7

- place one of your counters on that number on the grid.

Rule:
- If you can't find the answer on the grid, miss a go.

- The winner is the first player to get 3 of their counters in a line. A line can go sideways, up or down, or diagonally.

Subtract the dice

A game for 2 players

You need:
- two 0–9 dice
- counters in two different colours

Before you start:
- Each player choose a set of coloured counters.

Take turns to:
- roll the dice
- take the smaller number away from the larger number and say the answer

> 7 take away 3 is 4

- place one of your counters on that number on the grid.

Rule:
- If you can't find the answer on the grid, miss a go.

- The winner is the first player to get 3 of their counters in a line. A line can go sideways, up or down, or diagonally.

6	7	4	8	6	12
3	1	5	7	9	2
10	4	2	3	7	6
0	8	1	5	10	4
8	5	7	3	0	9
2	9	1	6	5	11

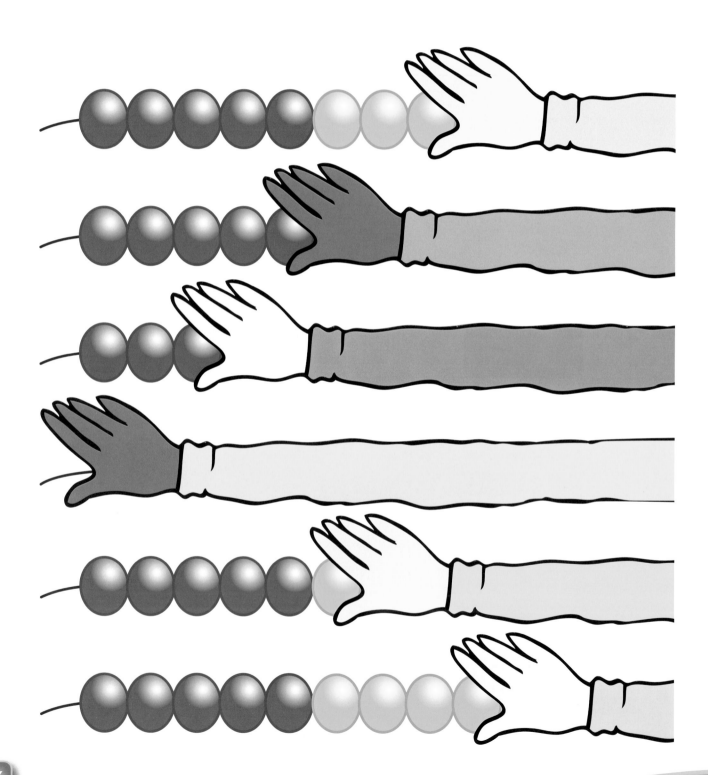

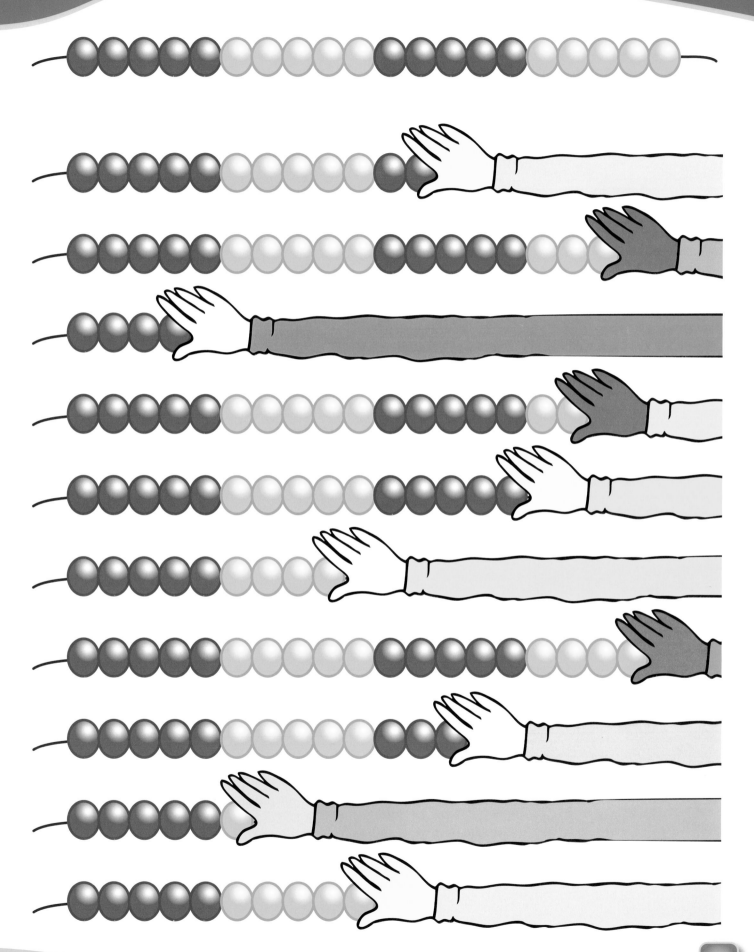

$6 + 8 = 14$

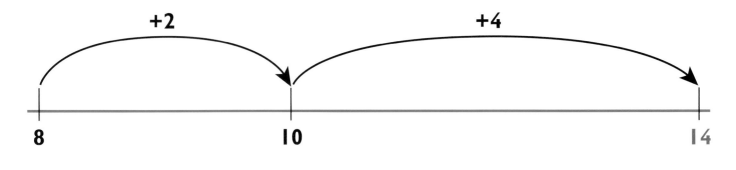

$7 + 9 = 16$

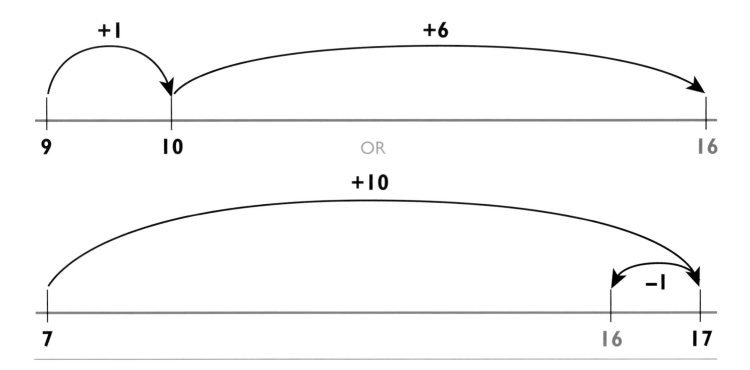

OR

$8 + 4 = 12$

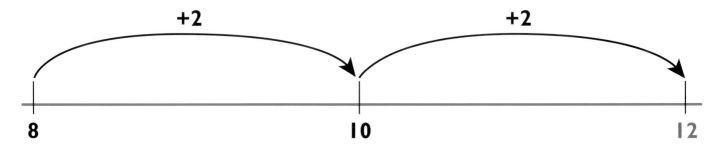

28 + 7 = 35

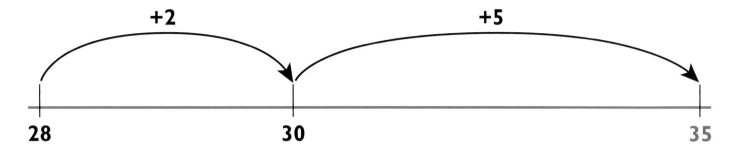

46 + 5 = 51

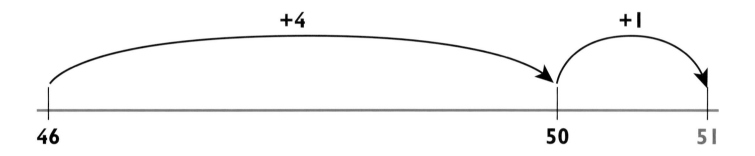

97 + 6 = 103

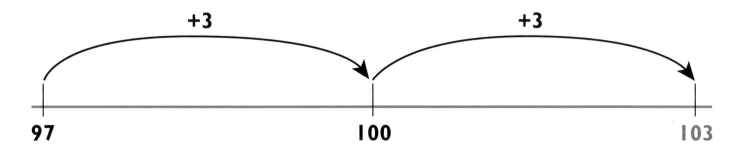

76 + 40 = 116

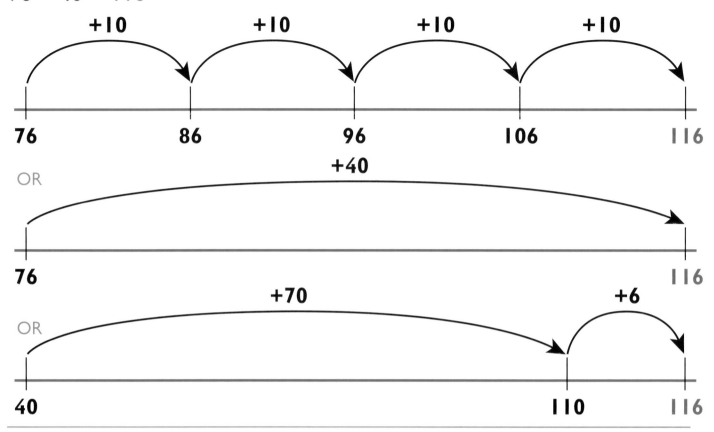

50 + 45 = 95

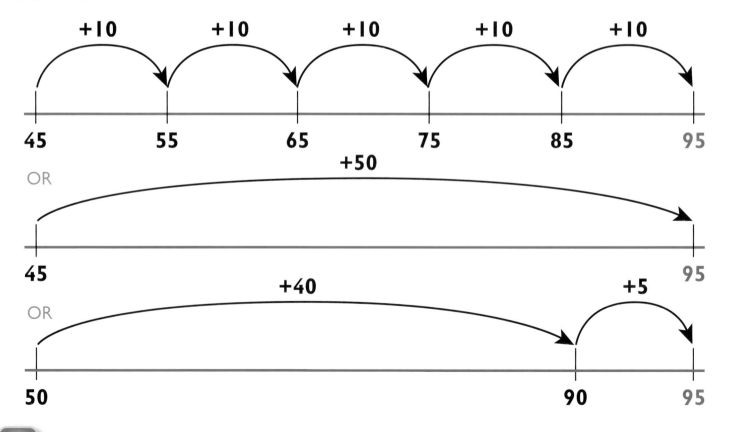

Remember

- Addition can be done in any order, so 77 + 46 is the same as 46 + 77
- Put the larger number first
- Count on the number of tens in the smaller number
- Count on the number of units in the smaller number

38 + 25 = 63

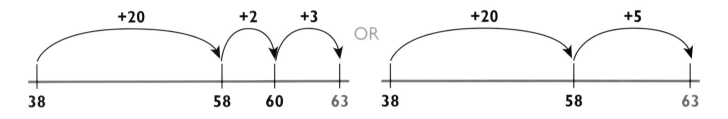

OR

$$38 + 25 = 38 + 20 + 5$$
$$= 58 + 5$$
$$= 63$$

$$38 + 25 = 30 + 20 + 8 + 5$$
$$= 50 + 13$$
$$= 63$$

$$\begin{array}{r} 30 + 8 \\ + \ 20 + 5 \\ \hline 50 + 13 = 63 \end{array}$$

46 + 77 = 123

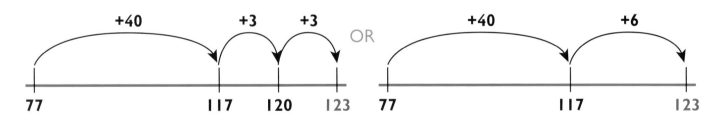

OR

$$77 + 46 = 77 + 40 + 6$$
$$= 117 + 6$$
$$= 123$$

$$77 + 46 = 70 + 40 + 7 + 6$$
$$= 110 + 13$$
$$= 123$$

$$\begin{array}{r} 70 + 7 \\ + \ 40 + 6 \\ \hline 110 + 13 = 123 \end{array}$$

8 − 3 = 5

● counting back

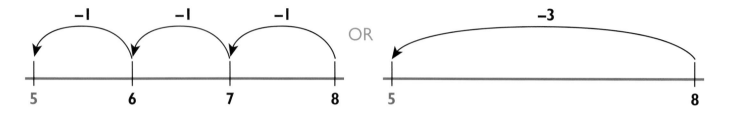

● counting up

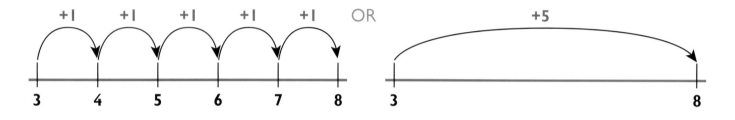

9 − 5 = 4

● counting back

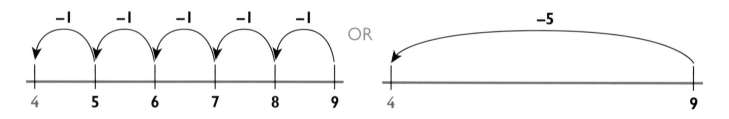

● counting up

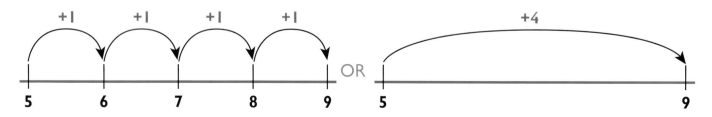

Remember

You can work out the answer to a subtraction number sentence by:

● counting back (take away) or

● counting up (find the difference).

34 − 6 = 28

● counting back

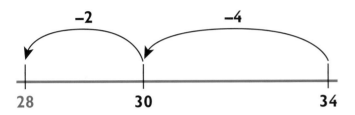

● counting up

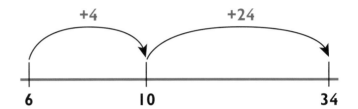

53 − 7 = 46

● counting back

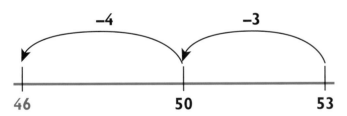

● counting up

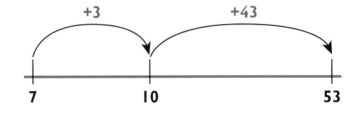

82 − 8 = 74

● counting back

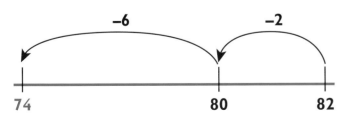

● counting up

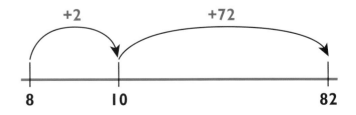

Remember

You can work out the answer to a subtraction number sentence by:

- counting back (take away) or
- counting up (find the difference).

52 − 30 = 22

- counting back

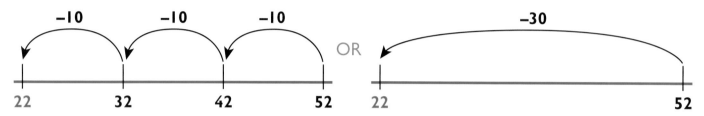

- counting up

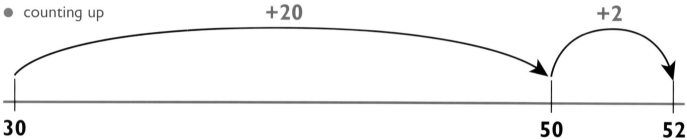

76 − 50 = 26

- counting back

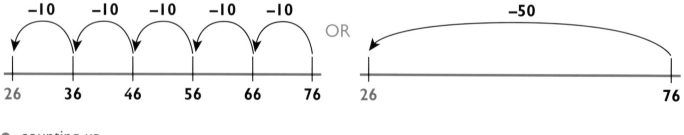

- counting up

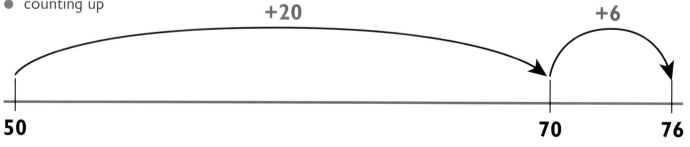

Remember

You can work out the answer to a subtraction number sentence by:
- counting back (take away) or
- counting up (find the difference).

42 – 27 = 15

- counting back

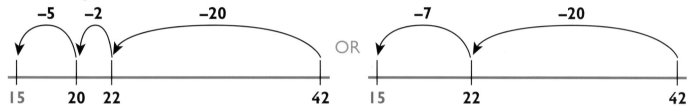

42 – 27 = 42 – 20 – 7
= 22 – 7
= 15

42 – 27 = 40 + 2 – 20 – 7
= 30 + 12 – 20 – 7
= 10 + 5
= 15

- counting up

73 – 45 = 28

- counting back

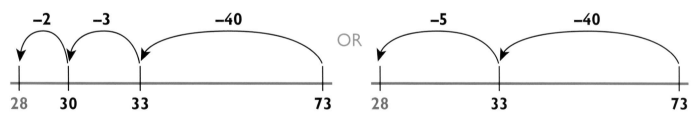

- counting up

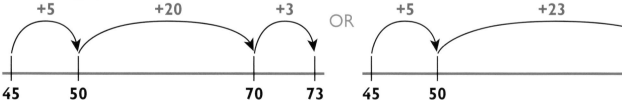

73 – 45 = 73 – 40 – 5
= 33 – 5
= 28

73 – 45 = 70 + 3 – 40 – 5
= 60 + 13 – 40 – 5
= 20 + 8
= 28

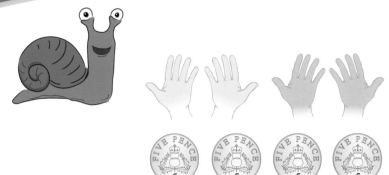

5×4

$5 + 5 + 5 + 5$

$5p + 5p + 5p + 5p$

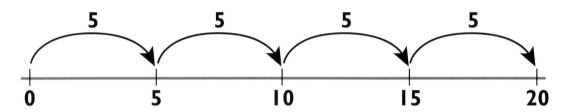

5	5	5	5
0	5	10	15	20

10×5

$10 + 10 + 10 + 10 + 10$

$10p + 10p + 10p + 10p + 10p$

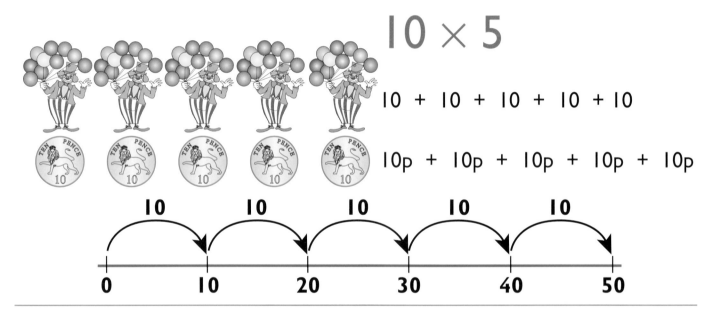

10	10	10	10	10
0	10	20	30	40	50

2×6

$2 + 2 + 2 + 2 + 2 + 2$

$2p + 2p + 2p + 2p + 2p + 2p$

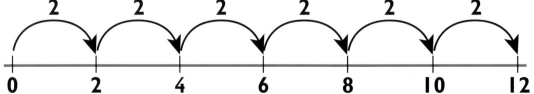

2	2	2	2	2	2
0	2	4	6	8	10	12

4 × 3 = 12

3 × 4 = 12

3 × 4 = 12

4 × 3 = 12

3 jumps of 4

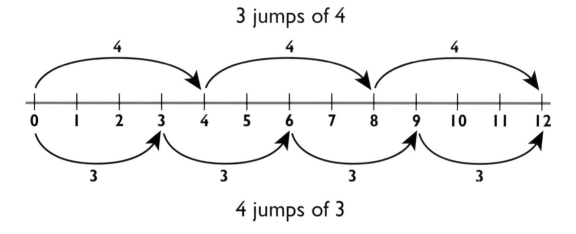

4 jumps of 3

3 × 2 = 6

2 × 3 = 6

2 × 3 = 6

3 × 2 = 6

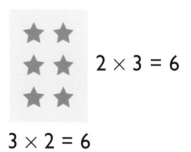

2 jumps of 3

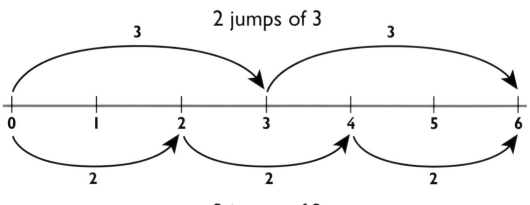

3 jumps of 2

2 times-table key facts

$1 \times 2 = 2$

$2 \times 2 = 4$

$5 \times 2 = 10$

$10 \times 2 = 20$

5 times-table key facts

$1 \times 5 = 5$

$2 \times 5 = 10$

$5 \times 5 = 25$

$10 \times 5 = 50$

10 times-table key facts

$1 \times 10 = 10$

$2 \times 10 = 20$

$5 \times 10 = 50$

$10 \times 10 = 100$

Player 1	**2 times-table**

6	→ ◯	20	→ ◯
14	→ ◯	12	→ ◯
16	→ ◯	8	→ ◯
10	→ ◯	2	→ ◯
4	→ ◯	18	→ ◯

Player 2	**2 times-table**

4	→ ◯	10	→ ◯
18	→ ◯	2	→ ◯
6	→ ◯	8	→ ◯
20	→ ◯	12	→ ◯
16	→ ◯	14	→ ◯

Player 1 **5 times-table**

45	→ ◯	20	→ ◯
10	→ ◯	35	→ ◯
40	→ ◯	5	→ ◯
25	→ ◯	30	→ ◯
15	→ ◯	50	→ ◯

Player 2 **5 times-table**

20	→ ◯	30	→ ◯
10	→ ◯	5	→ ◯
35	→ ◯	50	→ ◯
45	→ ◯	40	→ ◯
25	→ ◯	15	→ ◯

Player 1 — **10 times-table**

60 ⟶ ◯   40 ⟶ ◯

10 ⟶ ◯   80 ⟶ ◯

50 ⟶ ◯   20 ⟶ ◯

100 ⟶ ◯   90 ⟶ ◯

30 ⟶ ◯   70 ⟶ ◯

Player 2 — **10 times-table**

40 ⟶ ◯   20 ⟶ ◯

100 ⟶ ◯   70 ⟶ ◯

60 ⟶ ◯   80 ⟶ ◯

90 ⟶ ◯   10 ⟶ ◯

50 ⟶ ◯   30 ⟶ ◯

Player 1 — **Dividing by 2**

6 ÷ 2 → ◯	20 ÷ 2 → ◯
14 ÷ 2 → ◯	12 ÷ 2 → ◯
16 ÷ 2 → ◯	8 ÷ 2 → ◯
10 ÷ 2 → ◯	2 ÷ 2 → ◯
4 ÷ 2 → ◯	18 ÷ 2 → ◯

Player 2 — **Dividing by 2**

4 ÷ 2 → ◯	10 ÷ 2 → ◯
18 ÷ 2 → ◯	2 ÷ 2 → ◯
6 ÷ 2 → ◯	8 ÷ 2 → ◯
20 ÷ 2 → ◯	12 ÷ 2 → ◯
16 ÷ 2 → ◯	14 ÷ 2 → ◯

Player 1 · **Dividing by 5**

40 ÷ 5 → ◯   20 ÷ 5 → ◯

10 ÷ 5 → ◯   35 ÷ 5 → ◯

45 ÷ 5 → ◯   5 ÷ 5 → ◯

25 ÷ 5 → ◯   30 ÷ 5 → ◯

15 ÷ 5 → ◯   50 ÷ 5 → ◯

Player 2 · **Dividing by 5**

20 ÷ 5 → ◯   30 ÷ 5 → ◯

10 ÷ 5 → ◯   5 ÷ 5 → ◯

35 ÷ 5 → ◯   50 ÷ 5 → ◯

45 ÷ 5 → ◯   40 ÷ 5 → ◯

25 ÷ 5 → ◯   15 ÷ 5 → ◯

Player 1 — Dividing by 10

60 ÷ 10 → ◯   40 ÷ 10 → ◯
10 ÷ 10 → ◯   80 ÷ 10 → ◯
50 ÷ 10 → ◯   20 ÷ 10 → ◯
100 ÷ 10 → ◯   90 ÷ 10 → ◯
30 ÷ 10 → ◯   70 ÷ 10 → ◯

Player 2 — Dividing by 10

40 ÷ 10 → ◯   20 ÷ 10 → ◯
100 ÷ 10 → ◯   70 ÷ 10 → ◯
60 ÷ 10 → ◯   80 ÷ 10 → ◯
90 ÷ 10 → ◯   10 ÷ 10 → ◯
50 ÷ 10 → ◯   30 ÷ 10 → ◯

12 × 6

60p

12p

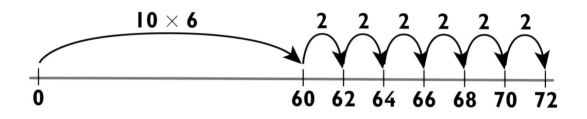

OR

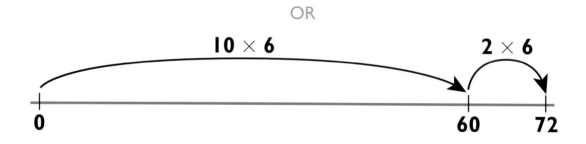

$$12 \times 6 = (10 \times 6) + (2 \times 6)$$
$$= 60 + 12$$
$$= 72$$

×	10	2	
6	60	12	= 72

25 × 7

140p

35p

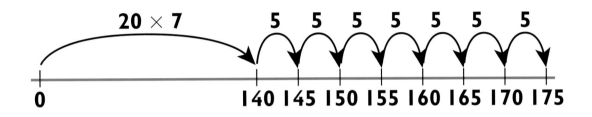

OR

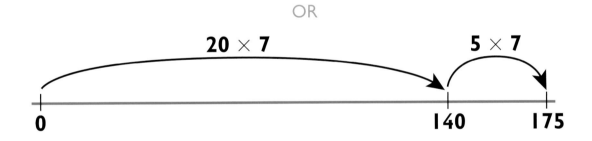

$$25 \times 7 = (20 \times 7) + (5 \times 7)$$
$$= 140 + 35$$
$$= 175$$

×	20	5	
7	140	35	= 175

56 ÷ 5

10   1 R 1 = 11 R 1

5 | 50 | 6   ➡   5 | 50 | 6

```
        56
       ↙  ↘
     50  +  6
      ↓      ↓     ÷ 5
     10  +  1 R 1 = 11 R 1
```

56 ÷ 5 = (50 + 6) ÷ 5
       = (50 ÷ 5) + (6 ÷ 5)
       = 10 + 1 R 1
       = 11 R 1

---

78 ÷ 2

20   19 = 39

2 | 40 | 38   ➡   2 | 40 | 38   OR

35   4   = 39

2 | 70 | 8   ➡   2 | 70 | 8

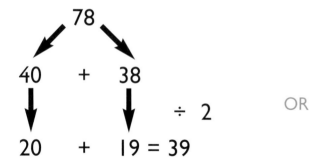

```
        78
       ↙  ↘
     40  +  38
      ↓      ↓     ÷ 2
     20  +  19 = 39
```

OR

```
        78
       ↙  ↘
     70  +  8
      ↓      ↓     ÷ 2
     35  +  4 = 39
```

78 ÷ 2 = (40 + 38) ÷ 2
       = (40 ÷ 2) + (38 ÷ 2)
       = 20 + 19
       = 39

OR   78 ÷ 2 = (70 + 8) ÷ 2
            = (70 ÷ 2) + (8 ÷ 2)
            = 35 + 4
            = 39

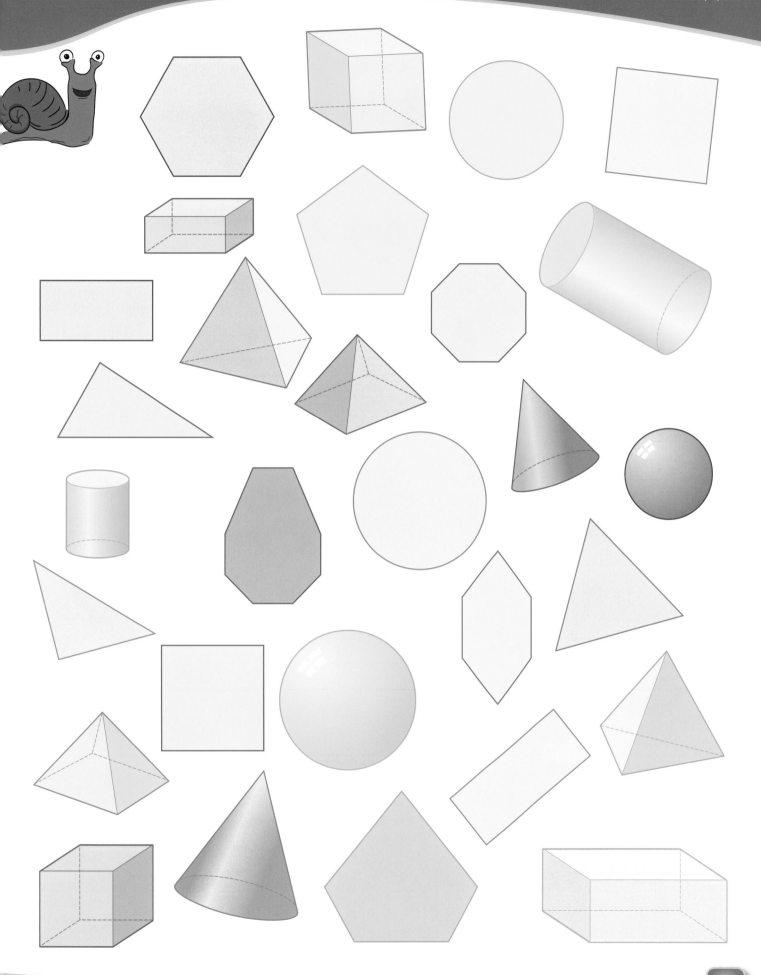

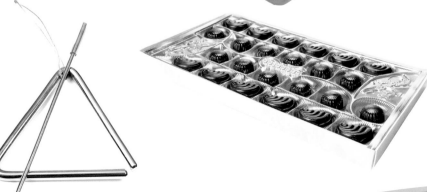

STOP

2-D shape names

A game for 2 players

You need:
- pencil and paper clip, for the spinner
- 25 counters

Take turns to:
- spin the **blue** spinner
- place a counter on that shape on the grid.

- The winner is the first player to complete a line of 4 counters. A line can go sideways, up or down, or diagonally.

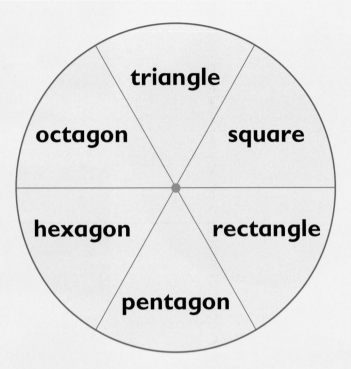

2-D shape sides and corners

A game for 2 players

You need:
- pencil and paper clip, for the spinner
- 25 counters

Take turns to:
- spin the **red** spinner
- find a shape on the grid with that many sides or corners, and cover it with a counter
- say the name of the shape.

- The winner is the first player to complete a line of 4 counters. A line can go sideways, up or down, or diagonally.

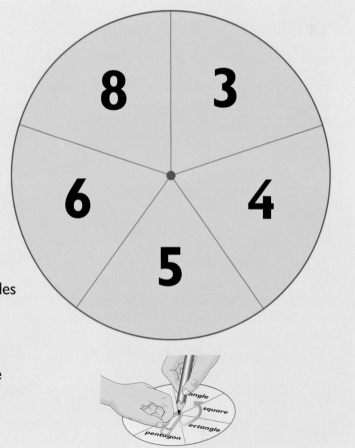

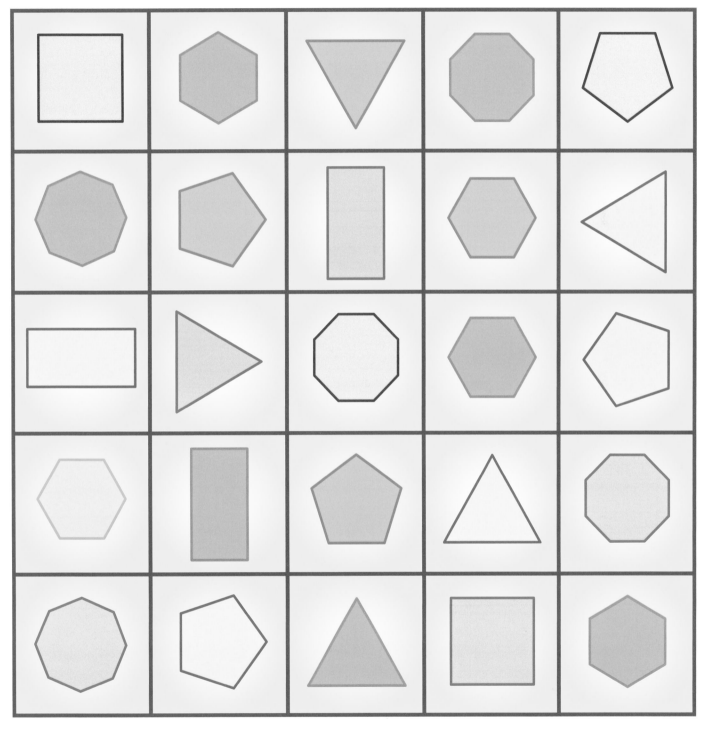

3-D solid names

A game for 2 players

You need:
- pencil and paper clip, for the spinner
- 25 counters

Take turns to:
- spin the **blue** spinner
- place a counter on that solid on the grid.

- The winner is the first player to complete a line of 4 counters. A line can go sideways, up or down, or diagonally.

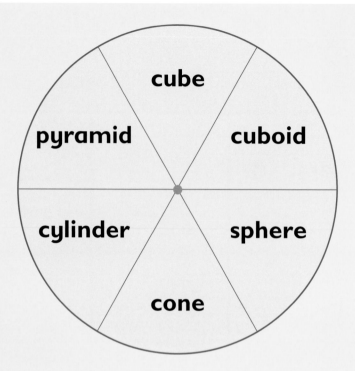

3-D solid faces

A game for 2 players

You need:
- pencil and paper clip, for the spinner
- 25 counters

Take turns to:
- spin the **red** spinner
- find a solid on the grid with that many faces, and cover it with a counter
- say the name of the solid.

- The winner is the first player to complete a line of 4 counters. A line can go sideways, up or down, or diagonally.

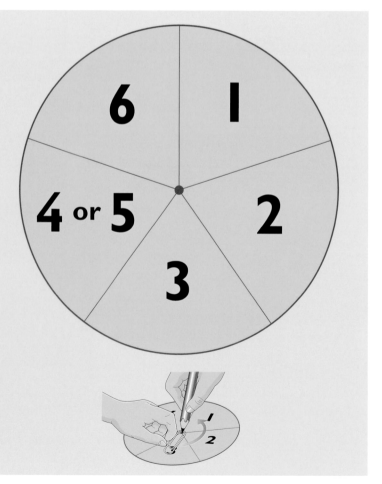

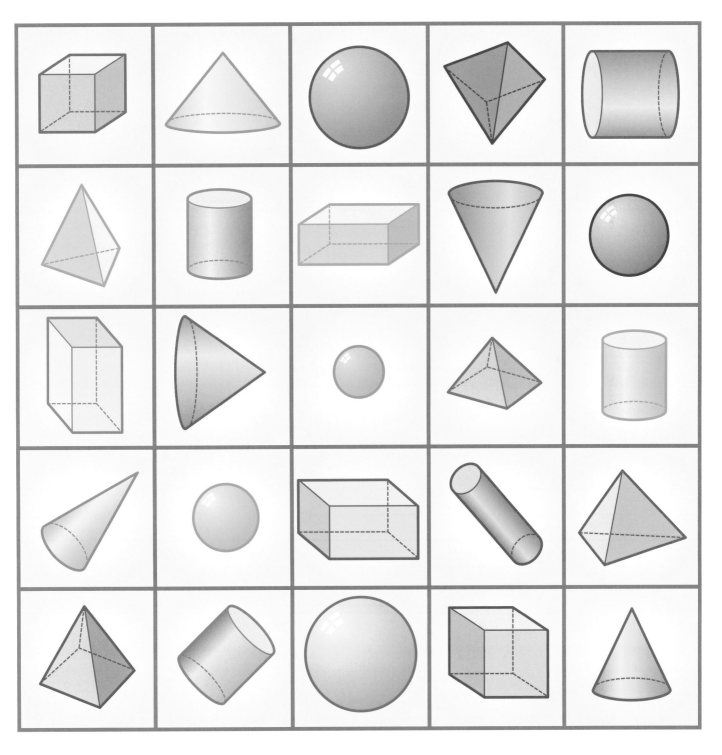

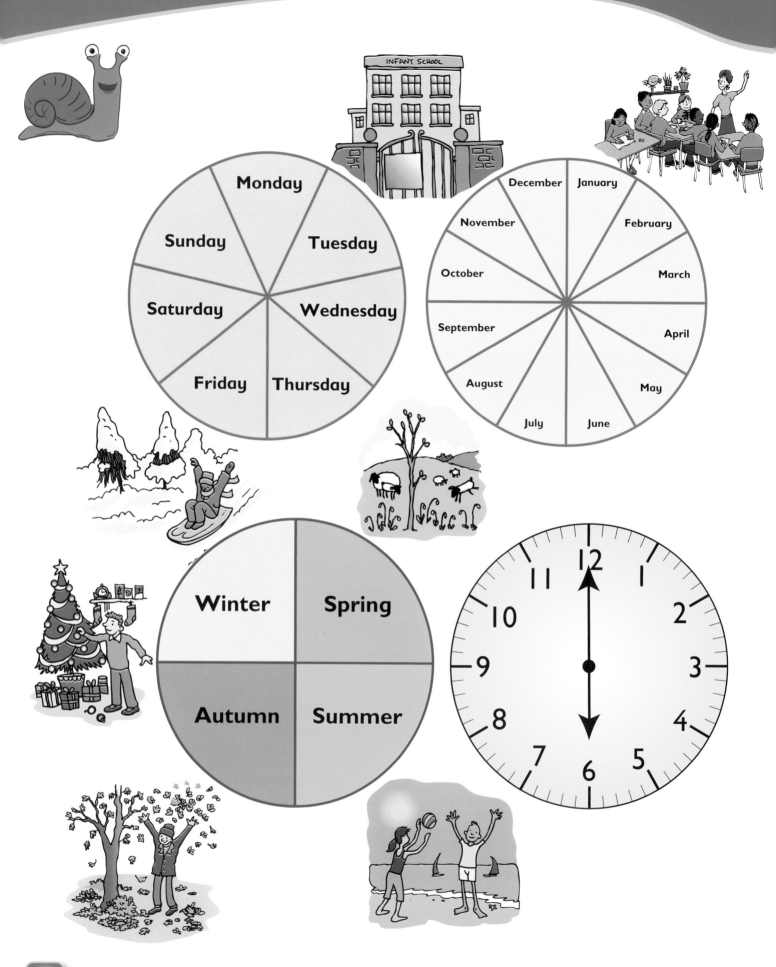

Monday

Tuesday

Wednesday

Thursday

Friday

Saturday

Sunday

December January February March April May June July August September October November

Winter Spring Summer Autumn

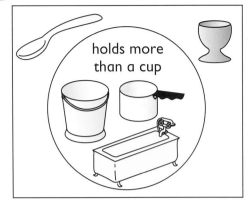

holds more than a cup

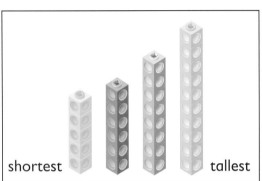

shortest   tallest

has 4 corners

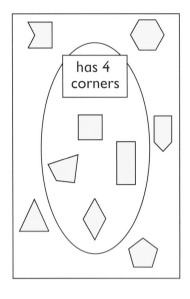

multiples of 2	
less than 20	20 or more
4	22
6	26
10	30
12	38
18	44

Vehicles we saw

type	number
car	24
motorbike	16
bicycle	10
bus	3
van	8
truck	4

one-digit numbers	not one-digit numbers
5 7 8 6 2 4 3 9 1	15 20 16 42 58 87 103

name	age
Grant	7 years 2 months
Lee	6 years 9 months
Paula	7 years 7 months
Pinder	6 years 8 months
Rav	6 years 10 months
Oliver	6 years 8 months

bread
butter
milk
eggs
bananas
chocolate
chicken
beans
pasta

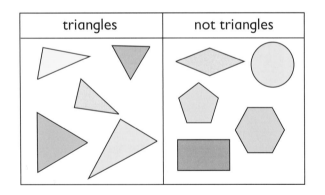

triangles	not triangles

heavier than me	not heavier than me

Our families

no brothers or sisters	1 brother or sister	2 brothers or sisters	3 brothers or sisters	more than 3 brothers or sisters
Peter Sue	Joe Rav Brian Amber	Olive Jake Joshua	David Lisa Sundus	Hazim